Let Him That Is without Sin . . .

Extending the Grace of Forgiveness for Moral Failure

by
Tom Allen

CHRISTIAN PUBLICATIONS, INC.
CAMP HILL, PENNSYLVANIA

3825 Hartzdale Dr.
Camp Hill, Pennsylvania 17011
www.cpi-horizon.com

ISBN: 0-87509-748-0

Printed in the United States of America

98 99 00 01 02 5 4 3 2 1

Let Him That Is without Sin . . .

My fax machine generally delivers rather benign, unemotional news. I usually receive reports, flight schedules, meeting agendas and other general information. But about a month before I wrote this booklet, a very troubling fax was transmitted through the telephone lines. I was informed of the moral failure and subsequent resignation of a prominent Christian leader. And it was someone I knew. Someone I had laughed with and prayed with and served with.

For me, this tragic news was the culmination of several spiritual wrecks along the ministry highway over the past nine months. It no longer resembled just one or two cars crashed along the road. Instead, it began to look more like a multi-car pileup I had seen along Interstate 75 in Chattanooga, Tennessee during a heavy fog. Bodies were strewn everywhere and vehicles were smashed as the resultant chain reaction took its toll.

This has been a sobering experience. I have been forced to pause and consider my own life. I'm in my "middle ministry years" right now, having served the Lord for twenty-one years. Hopefully, I'll have another twenty or twenty-five to give Him. There are some serious implications to mull over as I have observed my fallen brothers and sisters. And so I offer these reflections on moral failure to the whole body of Christ—full-time workers and lay people. This is for you. This is for me.

Process vs. Crisis

Moral failure is more often a gradual process than it is a sudden crisis.

Months, usually years, of smaller defeats in the moral arena lead to the major downfall. We tend to think of the messy bomb that explodes when the immorality goes public. But there is always that pesky fuse to consider. Sometimes it is a very long fuse. Once it is lit, there will be some opportunities to pinch it so that the explosion never occurs. However, that tragedy-saving pinch is often very difficult to execute.

King Solomon, the man of a thousand women, understood this process all too well:

> King Solomon, however, loved many foreign women besides Pharaoh's daughter. . . . They were from nations about which

the LORD had told the Israelites, "You must not intermarry with them, because they will surely turn your hearts after their gods." Nevertheless, Solomon held fast to them in love. He had seven hundred wives of royal birth and three hundred concubines, and his wives led him astray. As Solomon grew old, his wives turned his heart after other gods, and his heart was not fully devoted to the LORD his God, as the heart of David his father had been. (1 Kings 11:1-4)

Solomon talks about the difficulty of retracing one's steps once the process of seduction has begun:

With persuasive words she led
him astray;
she seduced him with her
smooth talk.
All at once he followed her
like an ox going to the slaughter,
like a deer stepping into a noose
till an arrow pierces his liver,
like a bird darting into a snare,
little knowing it will cost him
his life.

Now then, my sons, listen to me;
pay attention to what I say.
Do not let your heart turn to
her ways

or stray into her paths.
Many are the victims she has
brought down;
her slain are a mighty throng.
Her house is a highway to the
grave,
leading down to the cham-
bers of death.
(Proverbs 7:21-27)

Throughout Proverbs 5, 6 and 7, this truth emerges: Rarely does someone just suddenly decide to have an affair. Long conversations precede that first simple touch, the sensual caress and then the sexual act. It is a slow, often subtle operation: "With persuasive words she led him astray; she seduced him with her smooth talk." Games are played in the mind long before they are acted upon with the body. But there does seem to be a point along the way where the gradual slope suddenly drops off: "All at once he followed her." The challenge for all of us is to recognize this process in its infancy. Early detection can enable us to climb back up that gradual slope before we reach the cliff.

Moral failure, then, is usually a slow process leading to a sudden crisis. And there is a sense in which it is "too late" to rescue someone who has chosen to jump off that cliff. Once the will has been compromised in this direction, the incredibly strong allure of sexual pleasure will usually provide the final push. We must discover ways to identify those who are in the process of falling into this sin so that we can bring healing and recovery before the decision becomes irreversible.

Getting Caught

The person who commits to immoral behavior believes he or she will never get caught.

For reasons unknown, immorality is particularly susceptible to the fantasy of invincibility. Each one seems to feel that he or she will be the exception. *People get caught because they just aren't clever enough,* each thinks. *I can enjoy this sinful pleasure for a while, and then I'll just quit before anyone finds out.*

But the truth is this: Moral failure usually leads to sexual addiction. It's not usually the kind of sin that one can choose "for a while" and then suddenly "quit." The grip is a tight one that often leads to years of sexual sin. And the longer someone practices immorality, the odds of getting caught become greater each day. In the words of Moses: "You may be sure that your sin will find you out" (Numbers 32:23).

Solomon framed this reality in more graphic terms:

> Can a man scoop fire into his lap
> without his clothes being
> burned?

Can a man walk on hot coals
without his feet being
scorched?
So is he who sleeps with another man's wife;
no one who touches her will
go unpunished.
(Proverbs 6:27-29)

Assume for a moment that it is possible for a person to go throughout his or her entire life without "getting caught." There is still that one final checkpoint. And the implications are far more serious than any consequence faced in this world. Romans 14:10 and 12 declare in simple, undeniable terms that "we will all stand before God's judgment seat. . . . Each of us will give an account of himself to God."

With fear and trembling, let us acknowledge that ultimately everyone gets caught.

Ripple Effects

The ripple effect of moral failure is always larger than we think.

Perhaps this is the greatest cover-up our enemy uses to trap us in the arena of sexual temptation. Satan says, "This is no big deal. It's just between you and the other person. If you feel guilty afterward, you can confess it to each other, and no one will ever find out about it." He employs the same old trick he used at the very beginning: the minimization of sinful acts and their unavoidable consequences. Lucifer promised Eve, "You will not surely die" (Genesis 3:4).

In essence, the serpent was indicating that God was exaggerating the consequences for eating of the tree in the middle of the garden: "Who knows? It may even turn out to be a positive experience! You could end up with incredible insight and knowledge. But all this talk about death and devastation is just a scare tactic to make you obey. I say, 'Go for it!' "

But when moral failure hits the fan, there are immediate, enormous and far-reaching ripple effects. These consequences burst onto the scene like a dam breaking into a ferocious flood. Consider just a few of the people who are devastated when moral failure is uncovered:

- The spouses on both sides
- The children on both sides
- The parents and other extended family members
- Their church
- The new believers who are watching

When ministers and leaders succumb to moral failure, we can add the following ripple effects to the daunting list above:

- Other pastors, especially the younger ones just getting started

- Associates and staff members
- Parishioners
- Counselees

Galatians 6:7-8 addresses the issue of "ripple effect":

> Do not be deceived: God cannot be mocked. A man reaps what he sows. The one who sows to please his sinful nature, from that nature will reap destruction; the one who sows to please the Spirit, from the Spirit will reap eternal life.

Job refers to adultery as "a fire that burns to Destruction" (Job 31:12). Solomon tells us that the prostitute's house is "a highway to the grave, leading down to the chambers of death" (Proverbs 7:27). Surely there is no such thing as moral failure in a vacuum. The ripple effects are always larger than we think.

Finishing Well

Longevity does not guarantee a safe landing.

A misconception of young Christians goes something like this: "Temptation will decrease as I get older in the Lord. It will become easier to be holy as I mature. If I can just get through the early years without yielding to temptation, I can coast on in."

Unfortunately, this is not the case. In the majority of moral failure scenarios I have observed recently among friends in the ministry, these men had served the Lord for more than twenty-five years.

In the context of finishing well at the final resurrection, Paul urges us to remain vigilant about our walk with the Lord: "Therefore . . . stand firm. Let nothing move you. Always give yourselves fully to the work of the Lord, because you know that your labor in the Lord is not in vain" (1 Corinthians 15:58).

Peter offered similar advice to his brothers and sisters:

> Be self-controlled and alert. Your enemy the devil prowls around like a roaring lion looking for someone to devour. Resist him, standing firm in the faith. . . .Be on your guard so that you may not be carried away by the error of lawless men and fall from your secure position. But grow in the grace and knowledge of our Lord and Savior Jesus Christ. (1 Peter 5:8-9; 2 Peter 3:17-18)

Hopefully, we will become more skilled in coping with temptation as we walk with the Lord. But the notion of decreased intensity in spiritual warfare is a lie. And if God gives us a larger platform for ministry, we will become an even bigger target for the enemy. The devil would have much more to gain from the moral failure of a prominent layman, pastor, missionary, evangelist or district leader.

There is no safe time or place at any stage of the Christian life to "put down our guard" in the area of moral purity. None of us can afford the luxury of even one weak link in this chain. We have no margin for error. The number of years we have walked with the Lord will not, by themselves, protect us from moral failure. If we are to finish well, we must be diligent right to the end.

Amazing Grace

God's grace for forgiveness, healing and restoration is available for failures of every kind.

As heretical as this may sound, I'm not sure I have always believed this. Yes, I've given lip service to "amazing grace," but I have secretly considered a few sins to be in an "unpardonable" category. The person might still get to heaven if he or she humbly confessed and genuinely repented. But in my mind, his or her usefulness for God on this earth was over.

Thankfully, there has been a "grace awakening" in my life. This has been so refreshing. The Lord has broken me in new ways that have made me come up hungry for His grace in my own life. I've stepped down from the judge's chair. I no longer feel that it is my place to assess the status of fallen brothers and sisters who are seeking restoration. Paul's admonition has taken on new meaning for me: "Brothers, if someone is caught in a sin, you who are spiritual should restore him gently. . . . Carry each other's burdens, and in this way you will fulfill the law of Christ" (Galatians 6:1-2).

Of course, there must be real repentance. And moral failure does require a willingness to submit to the discipline of the church. But when these conditions have been met, we must forgive even as we have been forgiven. We must be willing to find new ministries for our restored brothers and sisters. Ignoring their spiritual gifts and desire to serve the Lord again is not an option. We must stop shooting our wounded.

I am thinking right now of a musician and a pastor who, after confessing their moral failure, have followed the prescribed path for reinstatement in their respective denominations. Both have returned to the same position in ministry. There was a time when I would have condemned this kind of restoration because I had a distorted view of God's great grace. But if the people involved with these individuals believe that they are ready to return, who am I to offer an opposing view?

It's dangerous to begin categorizing sin. "Well, if a person commits that sin, the Lord will put him on the shelf! He'll never be used of God again!" This is a very limited, unscriptural view of grace, forgiveness and the restorative powers of our Redeemer. The church has spent too much time and energy detailing and defending consequences for moral failure. We need to spend more time and energy finding ways to bring healing and restoration to those who have fallen. We should be looking for new ways to use these dear ones who have returned to the Lord.

The Integrity of the Church

When the church is honest about its sin, and when grace is properly extended to those who fall, the credibility of the gospel will not be harmed in the long run.

Many congregations are afraid to deal openly and honestly with the moral failure of a pastor or a lay person. It would appear that the safest, easiest approach is to sweep it under a rug. People will say things like, "Just think about the negative impact that this disclosure of immorality will have on the cause of Christ in our community!" But here's the real deal: It will have an extremely negative long-term impact in the community if we are dishonest and deceptive in dealing with this sin. And though openly and honestly confronting moral failure may have painful short-term repercussions, the gospel will not be harmed in the long run.

Make no mistake. Christianity is wounded when believers fall. But we can choose to act in ways that will minimize the negative impact. It's a very simple matter. If we "go by the Book" on this one, God will honor our candor. "He who conceals his sins does not prosper, but whoever confesses and renounces them finds mercy" (Proverbs 28:13).

All the ingredients must come together. Honesty in dealing with the immorality. Grace properly extended to the perpetrators. Then credibility can eventually be returned to the body of Christ.

A Warning

I am capable of moral failure, and so are you.

As I have reflected on this issue during these past several months, this has been the most frightening reality of all. I am capable of moral failure. And so are you.

I intentionally skipped a portion of Galatians 6:1 when I quoted it earlier. Now I'd like you to see the entire passage from Galatians 6:1-3:

> Brothers, if someone is caught in a sin, you who are spiritual should restore him gently. But watch yourself, or you also may

> be tempted. Carry each other's burdens, and in this way you will fulfill the law of Christ. If anyone thinks he is something when he is nothing, he deceives himself.

This passage will knock anyone off of the high horse of pride. In the very act of restoring others, the apostle indicates that we need to be aware of our own vulnerability and capacity for immorality: "Watch yourself, or you also may be tempted." And just to make sure he has hammered his point home, Paul reminds us that we can be deceived into thinking we are something when we are really nothing. This is not an attack on "self-worth"—it's a declaration of war against self-sufficiency in the arena of temptation.

So, one extreme could be summarized by the person who says, "I am not susceptible to moral failure." The other extreme would be to expect failure. Some who read this booklet may become overwhelmed by feelings of inadequacy and impending defeat. But we should not succumb to this level of hopelessness. A professor in college once offered this hope-filled advice to our class with regard to sin:

- Don't EXCITE sin
- Don't EXCUSE sin
- Don't EXPECT sin

Through the years, this has proven to be good advice. We should not be involved in those things that we know will "excite" sin. This is what Paul meant when he said we should "flee the evil desires of youth, and pursue righteousness" (2 Timothy 2:22). Also, we must never "excuse" sin when God reveals it to us. We should immediately confess it and turn from it. And we do not need to "expect" sin. This means that we should never give in to a defeatist mentality that anticipates failure on a regular basis.

To say that you and I are capable of moral failure is to humbly recognize our potential for immoral behavior. In the words of the old hymn:

> Prone to wander, Lord, I feel it,
> Prone to leave the God I love;
> Here's my heart, oh, take and
> seal it—
> Seal it for Thy courts above.

So we must guard our own hearts and minds. We must allow ourselves to be kept by God's power. "I . . . am convinced that he is able to guard what I have entrusted to him for that day" (2 Timothy 1:12).

It is not all God's responsibility, and it's not all ours. It is a joint responsibility. We must cooperate with the Holy Spirit by yielding our will and dedicating our minds and bodies to purity. The verb tenses here indicate that He will keep on guarding what we keep on entrusting to Him.

Conclusion: There Is Hope

The Promise Keepers' movement has revived an old scriptural principle that has the potential to rescue many from the tyranny and consequences of moral failure. There is hope. It can be found in the principle of accountability. The privatization of our culture has isolated one person from another, and this has led to a carnal individualism. It has also led to a great number of lonely men and women who struggle day after day in a private hell of temptation and despair.

We are commanded to "carry each other's burdens" in Galatians 6:2 because it is an evidence that we are serious about "fulfilling the law of Christ." ("Love your neighbor as yourself" is the specific law of Christ referred to here.) We must each find that person who will become a "soul mate"—someone with whom we can be totally honest about our struggles, temptations, failures and victories. I know from personal experience that this is not an easy assignment. But without this kind of biblical accountability, many—perhaps most—will find it difficult to avoid moral failure and its attending devastation.

Do you have this kind of accountability relationship with a confidante? I would encourage each reader to seek the Lord for just the right person—one who can be trusted with your deepest secrets. Some may be able to turn to a spouse in this way. For others, it will be more beneficial to share with someone from their own gender. However we choose to proceed, it's vital that we proceed. And the sooner, the better, because "As iron sharpens iron, so one man sharpens another" (Proverbs 27:17).

Praise God for the hope that can be offered to those who have already experienced moral failure! "If we confess our sins, he is faithful and just and will forgive us our sins and purify us from all unrighteousness" (1 John 1:9).

There is also hope for the person who can feel the strong downward pull of sexual temptation even though he or she has not surrendered to it:

> No temptation has seized you except what is common to man. And God is faithful; he will not let you be tempted beyond what you can bear. But when you are tempted, he will also provide a way out so that you can stand up under it. (1 Corinthians 10:13)

There is also hope for the brokenhearted loved ones, friends and associates of those who have fallen. "The LORD is close to the brokenhearted and saves those who are crushed in spirit" (Psalm 34:18).

Other Books/Booklets by Tom Allen

I Wish You Could Meet My Mom and Dad (1978)

Rock n' Roll, The Bible, and The Mind (1982)

Congregations in Conflict (1991)

Ten Foolish Things Christians Do to Stunt Their Growth (1996)

Joy Comes in the Mourning (1998)
(by David Johnson with Tom Allen)

"Spiritual Leadership Begins at Home"

Rev. Tom Allen is available to speak in churches, camps, retreats and schools. He can be contacted at:

Rev. Tom Allen
19368 180th Avenue
Big Lake, MN 55309
Phone/Fax: (612) 263-6711
E-mail: tomallenministries@juno.com